Fire's Goal

Fire's Goal

Poems from the Hindu Year

Laurie L. Patton

Illustrations by

Lika Tov

With a Foreword by

Narendra Panjwani

WHITE CLOUD PRESS
ASHLAND, OREGON

 Inquiries should be addressed to: White Cloud Press, PO Box 3400, Ashland, Oregon 97520. Website: www.whitecloudpress.com

Printed in Indonesia

First White Cloud Press edition: 2002

Cover design: David Rupee, Impact Publications

Poems from this volume have appeared previously in *ProVisions* ("Ganesh Chathurti"); *Mana Voori Maata* ("The Red Sparrow"; "Heirloom"); *Tmol Shilshom Literary Monthly* ("The Red-Throated Sparrow"); and *The Quadrangle* ("Sacred Thread"; "Fire's Goal"; "Widow's Bangles by the River Bed").

Library of Congress Cataloging-in-Publication Data

Patton, Laurie L., 1961-
Fire's Goal : poems from the Hindu year / Laurie L. Patton ;
illustrations by Lika Tov.
p. cm.
In English; some poems are in English and Sanskrit.
ISBN: 1-883991-49-8
1. Indic poetry (English)--20th century. I. Title

PR9495.7.P37 2003
821'.92--dc21

2002044928

Contents

Acknowledgments

Thank you to all readers: Ganesh Thite; Arshia Sattar; Kala Acharya; Maitreyee Deshpande; Wendy Doniger; Uma and Bhagirath Majmudar; Rachel McDermott; Gayatri Chatterjee; Paul Courtright; Jack Hawley; Tara Doyle; Parimal Patil; Paul Griffiths; Miranda Shaw; Anuradha Patra; Carolyn Wright; Joyce Fleuckiger; Barbara Patterson; Jose Cabezon; Edwin Bryant; Swami Yogeshananda; John Sitter; Gordon Newby; Alf Hiltebeitel; the Poetry Circle of Atlanta; Lynn Alexander; Daniel Veach; Callanwolde Arts Center; Indian American Cultural Association; Vedanta Center of Atlanta.

Special thanks to: Lika Tov; Franklin Lewis; Narendra Panjwani and Miriam Dosal; David Shulman; Steven Scholl; Nadine Berardi for Sanskrit refinements and corrections; and Shalom Goldman, best reader and best love.

In Memory of A. K. Ramanujan

Foreword

People construct such a variety of communities if given a chance, and they are even more creative when not given a chance. This book of poems looks likely to create another little community. Let's call them Hindu-Buddhist modernists, originating in the West, stretching to the East, and creating a new conversation about the meaning of Hindu India among readers on both sides of the Arabian Atlantic sea.

The author is a Boston Brahmin who has specialized in the Vedas, which are the canonical works of Hindu India. Most of us middle-class Indians have heard of, though not from, the Vedas. They are in an obscure early Sanskrit and we are in English (plus one or two contemporary local languages like Hindi, Urdu, Tamil, Bengali, etc.)

The poems are quite explicit about wanting to connect. "I want to remember," the author writes in her poem, "Dīwālī at Gangotri":

the flame floating down
in pure abstraction
oval orange heat
I want to recall
the mythical memory
of Bali crushed
Rāma in triumph,
encircling Sītā
but instead this small fire
encased by leaf
presses forward
by the violence of torrents
so that it finds its own eddies

The "I" in this poem, and the one which follows, is not the poet herself but the imagined devotee created by her.

Column of Light, Śivarātri

When the visitors arrived
I ran from the room
where your lights were

the guests sat sumptuous
at a distant table
where fruits and wines soaked them
and still your candles burned
indifferent to their feeding

your pillars of light
do not overwhelm
as do the mouths of caverns

they just endure
through wanton laughter
and careless feeding

they just confound
my anxious movements
with stubborn peace

What starts as a shock soon becomes a pleasure as the poems take us along on a passage through India. Here, the poet says, is Lord Ganeśa rounding off, softening the daily travels and travails of this rickshaw driver. And there, the stillness of Lord Śiva amidst the hubbub of celebration.

Modern middle class Indians live in an enchanted Hindu-Islamic-Buddhist-Christian world, but in a disenchanted way. The enchantment has been taken for granted by us, rendering it banal. But now here are poems which open our eyes, making the real strange once again. In poems like "Om Namaḥ Śivāya," the poet holds Śiva, and us, up, as subjects facing a large new mirror.

Wait, there is more. What we have here is the poet's relationship with the mirror. This is what the poems in this book are: an invitation to observe a relationship which is also a search on the poet's part. A search for the significance in the Hindu India she has adopted, a search for an imagination which can cross both worlds. It is not India as a nation, nor even Hinduism as a religion, but an environment, a structure of feeling, that makes an impact on poets. And poetry at its lyrical best deals with the imaginative aspect of that environment.

In keeping with this spirit, let me now end with an imaginative, even playful engagement with one with one particular poem–Hariścandra's promise to Viśvāmitra. This poem, because of its composition and tone, makes us rethink the hackneyed Hariścandra fable. Hariścandra is a king famous in Indian folklore for being an extreme do-gooder. When you want to reproach someone for his impractical altruism, you ask him to "stop being a bloody Hariścandra!"

This poem throws up an interesting Hindu question about Hariścandra: can we imagine detaching ourselves completely from wealth, home and family ties? Yes, those very things that constitute our identity, and start again from scratch? King Hariścandra did it, and he had a whole kingdom to lose. He did it, nonetheless, to fulfill a promise. The poem makes us realize that Hariścandra reinvented himself from this act, and became king of all time, a king who didn't need a kingdom anymore. Do we, enmeshed in upwardly mobile careers, washing machines, hi-tech multimedia PCs and 1000-watt sound systems, have the will to throw it all away? Are we willing, for all our unease with consumerism, to test for just a year, say, what it would be like? Why, we might ask, need we reinvent ourselves?

No compelling reason comes to mind. And yet, the mind wanders...and lands on a seemingly non Hindu passage in a nineteenth-century American novel about the deeds of a young heiress who suddenly comes into a lot of wealth. I refer to Edna Pontellier, the protagonist of Kate Chopin's novel, *The Awakening* (1899): "Every step which she took toward relieving herself from obligations added to her strength and expansion as an individual. She began to look with her own eyes; to see and to apprehend deeper undercurrents of life. No longer was she content to 'feed upon opinion' when her own soul had invited her." [Chopin, p.93, Ch. 32, in Margaret Culley's edition, New York: Norton, 1976]

Edna Pontellier, Chopin tells us, "even as a child . . . lived her own small life within herself. At a very early period she had apprehended instinctively the dual life—that outward existence which conforms, the inward life which questions." [ch 7., p.15, ibid] To the Indian ear, this would be so Hindu!

Strange, how the impulse to detachment from worldly ties, how forms of feeling, not just the feelings themselves, touch each other across continents, languages, cultures. Edna and Hariścandra, had they crossed paths while walking through Benares one evening (or Boston for that matter), might well have had a lot to say to each other.

In what sense then, I can almost hear Edna and Harish saying from on high, is the Diwali festival or Lord Ganeśa only Indian? If the impulse to detachment from worldly ties can be found in the Buddha, Hariścandra, and Edna in Christian Victorian England, then why are we so possessive about Indian gods, fables and festivals? We may not be able to detach ourselves from our Indianness, but why can't others partake of it too?

Similarly, the Dīwālī poem finds (and creates) special significance in a small flame floating precariously down a river on a leaf. No other poem has seen the Dīwālī festival quite like this. Harish (Edna's 'Harry' from their second meeting in Benares/Boston onwards) would have liked the poem, as much as Edna and we. So would Gautam Buddha and Virginia Woolf, as is evident if we listen to the character Bernard's very Hindu-Buddhist sounding observations on 'levels of reality' in her novel, *The Waves.*

In sum, when Harry met Edna, and Gautam Virginia, and talked so well with each other, and that was centuries ago, why are we twenty-first century global villagers sitting here worrying about religions, nations and borders? Let governments do that, if they must. . . .

Narendra Panjwani
Bombay, 2002

Preface

"Fire's Goal" is the name of a poem about the sage Śarabhanga, who consumed himself in fire because he could not stand to be in absence of the Lord Rama, who had ascended to heaven without him. The book, too, is about the consuming fire of longing, in God's presence and in God's absence. It is a kind of early twenty-first century *bhakti*, or devotional voice, in which the fire of longing consumes the one who longs in ways that are both specific to the contemporary devotee and also accessible to the non-Hindu reader.

These poems also reflect a year of journeys to sacred river sources in India—the icebergs of Gaumukh, the wells and ponds of Varanasi, the caves of Triambak and riverbanks of Nasik. They were written after a decade of writing and reading in interpretation of its most sacred Sanskrit compositions — the Veda.

The first half of the book, "Festivals," follows the main festivals of a Hindu year. Each poem is written in the voice of a *bhakta*, or devotee. Each attempts to portray a moment in the mind of such a person as he or she performs rituals of devotion—whether it be floating a flame down the river at Dīwālī or listening to the bell at a Ganeśa temple at Ganeśotsav. The first half might be called a phenomenological portrait of a Hindu year. There are many more festivals in the Hindu year than are included in this book–the calendar provides us with an embarrassment of riches which I only touch upon lightly here.

The second half of the book, "Crossings," refers to the traditional term *tīrtha*, or holy place. In India, a *tīrtha* is a place where a god crossed over to be on earth. “Crossings” employs the images of Sanskrit learning to think about ordinary moments in contemporary life—a lost lover, running with dogs, an encounter with a spider-web, what a widow might say about her broken bangles. I composed the last six poems in a simple form of the language of Sanskrit itself—without meter, and without reference to classical forms—to create a kind of Haiku of emotion. They are given in both Sanskrit and English.

With images from such texts and landscapes, then, this book is an attempt to create a Hindu world which opens up experiential and moral possibilities. It also addresses changes and transitions, and speaks about them in Hindu terms. These poems are an attempt to make the early twenty-first century experience of Hindu symbols and Sanskrit learning accessible from a perspective of tension and movement, approach and avoidance, the stuff of interaction with the contemporary world.

Fire's Goal takes for granted that each Hindu god is a poetically accessible being, who can elicit moods and moments which a non-Hindu might comprehend, appreciate, and be transformed by. In this sense, the use of Hindu mythology in this book is inspired by H.D., as well as many of the other symbolist poets, who used mythological referents in order to enrich and enliven their imagery and the experience of the reader.

The god of every Hindu festival, no matter how small in stature and scale, is a form of incompletion that begs to be completed by the experience of a devotee. Each festival, each god, points to a larger whole, which then must in turn become absorbed into some form of practice and experience. We can often speak of god in such a way that the whole takes absolute precedence, and the part must also refer to and become subsumed by it. But in a world of multiple divinities, the part often takes precedence, in constant deference to and interaction with the whole.

This idea (Ashis Nandy's “Hinduism for a postmodern age”), creates a challenge and opportunity for literary forms in writing about and through the gods of India. There is nothing romantic about the harsh challenge of a multiple form of divinity. In the liberal economy of India where everything is promised as “realizable” through interaction with and resistance to the idea of the “contemporary,” a deity stands as the epitome of such ambivalence. Deities promise the world, and yet they also withhold it. Gods embody both presence and absence in unique ways–ways which can teach us as much about contemporary lives as ancient ones.

Finally, this book also assumes that not everyone can understand the various nuances and cultural references which make up the poetry. It is impossible to assume a universal set of unspoken cultural referents; indeed, to me it is better not to opt for total cultural transparency. It seems right at this historical moment to use referents from different cultures in order to challenge the medium of English as one is using it. Thus I have tried to walk a middle path between transparency and resistance, providing footnotes and longer notes at the back to help the reader if further information is required.

Laurie L. Patton
Atlanta, GA 2002

Part 1

Festivals

Pūrṇimā,[1]
(Full Moon Sacrifice)

In this warming sky
you are fully white
needing white honor:
rice and boiled milk—
these are the ways

But the law
that white produces white
is not all there is
to your pull:

a cow's eye
looks back at the dawn
and traces your disappearance
in the sweeps of her tail;
the cooking pot
states a sphere
between sharp flames;

these are not copies
but so many fragments
craving your whole

I must remind you
to gather them up again
in whiteness

Śrāvaṇa, Nāga Pañcamī[2]

(Festival of Patañjali The Grammarian, Descended from the Snake)

This morning, you coil around
the last of sleep
hardly black, barely green
I cannot read you
between the blades of *kuśa* grass
between the leaves of palm

all days this month
you swim up to the light
defying your home
you twist around a doorpost
lace between fingers
children squint to find you

but you will tell me
squinting is necessary;
reading is beyond
the slither of letters
that catch the eye
and curl the tongue

you will say
it is unruly motion
between water and light
that makes rows of verbs
and strings of phrases

you will show
that my algae of words
cannot gleam
until you swim between them
slippery and clarifying.

Ganeśa Bell at Ganeśotsav

(Festival of the Elephant-Headed God of Thresholds)[3]

—for Raghu

Roundness keeps crossing
the lines of routine:
plants and children
blur the courtyard edges,
wash rags encircle
the tea-house tables,
fat rains interrupt
the black lines of my rickshaw

Even the tiles of your temple,
Lord, have stencils;
moons and creepers
snake through
blocks of clean white

Every day I ring your bell
before setting off to drive:
I make a round-bellied sound,
cutting through geometries
of carts and streets—
a curved ringing,
so that my prayers
—small square gifts of voice—
are always changing
in its leftover shimmers

your sound always changes
so that all lines are kept
and all lines are crossed—
so that everything is possible
at some moment or other

Kṛṣṇa Jayantī

(Festival of Kṛṣṇa, Cowherd and Consort of Lovers)[4]

What love
stands so tall and dark
what mahogany pleasure
bringing the peace
of a floating child

it is me and
yet it is not me
that you crave
your dark head bent
hungering for strength

my strength and yet also your own:
do not kiss
do not take up that music
until you tell me how you slept
and rested on the leaves
before you were so strong

Cycle of Hymns to the Goddess[5]

I. Mohenjodaro-Devī, Daśaharā
(Festival of the Goddess)

Mother, you are not Music:
these desert hymns drone[6]
pitched and lilting
but your hum glides
under their notes

you make muffled thunder
like the rolling of buffalo[7]
but you are stronger
more silent than them
their hooves stop, waiting,
while you turn and murmur

once when the buffaloes were gone
and the hymn-singers sleeping
I listened for you
between the dry furrows;
my ear pressed low
in burning biers of earth
I heard you crooning again

II. Lakṣmī Pūjā
(Festival of the Goddess of Wealth)

Last evening, cycling home,
the rack dragged sugarcane
under the bypass
and the evening before
it carried radishes
over the bridge

vegetables change shape
less easily than you,
spiraling Lakṣmī,
but they remind me
as my spokes hum
that while you traffic
in butter and flowers,
and turn them into coins
which mothers hold fast
in urgent dreaming,
my alchemy is similar:

the turning of sweat
born of radishes and sugar
into something dreamt—
something urgent—
like food

III. Sūr Khaṇḍa Devī Yatra,[8] Daśaharā

(Festival of the Goddess)

Mother, you are not Plenty
but a thin and grueling grace
just when I think
I might hold you
swollen and rounded
by coconuts and songs

you vanish into the gilt
of the pujāri's pages
and play, reed-like,
between the sticks of incense
you slip into the cement
still resounding with bells

just when I think
I have arranged my breasts
to match the fullness of yours
you become a small wind
blowing glimpses of red cloth
all the way up the mountain.

IV. Piṭhorī, Hymn to the Seven Mothers[9]

Mother, you are not birth
but half-birth:
listen as I tell you,
stopped at this temple
building my fruit offerings:

my name is Videhā,
I have no body
or else too much body
I bled eight children
flesh that did not breathe

But look, mother:
I have made lack a virtue:
pots—clay wombs—
arranged before you,
and seven flour statues
in all your forms.

My flour cannot breathe,
but it can signify
and it can increase
while flesh only gives way
to breathlessness.

With this flour
I will call you
by all of your names
and you will answer
piece by piece

you will re-assemble
this body of half-births
into a towering whole.

Brāhmī,[10] fill my mouth
with searing speech
singing labor songs
as the child kicks
its way toward breath

Māheśvarī,[11] brass goddess
ring metal bells
filling my ears
as the labor song runs

Kaumārī,[12] wife of battle
hold my back
where the spear strikes
as the child crowns

Vaiṣṇavī,[13] make your omens
arcs in the sky
so that I can see them
as I arch upward

Vārāhī,[14] you have held
the earth before;
make it still
as the child falls

Indrāṇī,[15] play with him
flirt and run
so that he is teased
into breathing

Chāmuṇḍā,[16] leatherworker,
wrap him in your skin
so that he knows
the feel of covering

All of you, seven mothers
name this birthing body
claim this flesh as your own

perhaps then
named by you
he will stay
beating your rhythms
breathing your songs
he will be an offering

and I, Videhā,
will lose my name
to another glory.

Dīwālī at Gangotri[17]

I want to remember
the flame floating down
in pure abstraction
oval, orange, heat
I want to recall
the mythical memory
of Bali crushed,[18]
Rāma in triumph,
encircling Sītā[19]

but instead this small fire
encased by leaf
presses forward
by the violence of torrents
so that it finds its own eddies

still small, it starts down
ten thousand feet
I blink as I imagine
how it might survive

no mythical memory here
just the sheerness of drop
and the chance that the victory
of light over darkness
is neither in memory
nor abstraction

but in that mother's eye
as she climbs to her temple,
listens to the river
and glimpses the flame

in the flinch of the yogi[20]
who breathes in the night
and sees the pale flash
between snow and bamboo

in the mistake by the child
who thinks it a shell
and reaches into the river
to hold the glow near

light over darkness
brings triumph of motion
perpetual distraction
and perceptual error

before its leaf
finally succumbs
to the waves

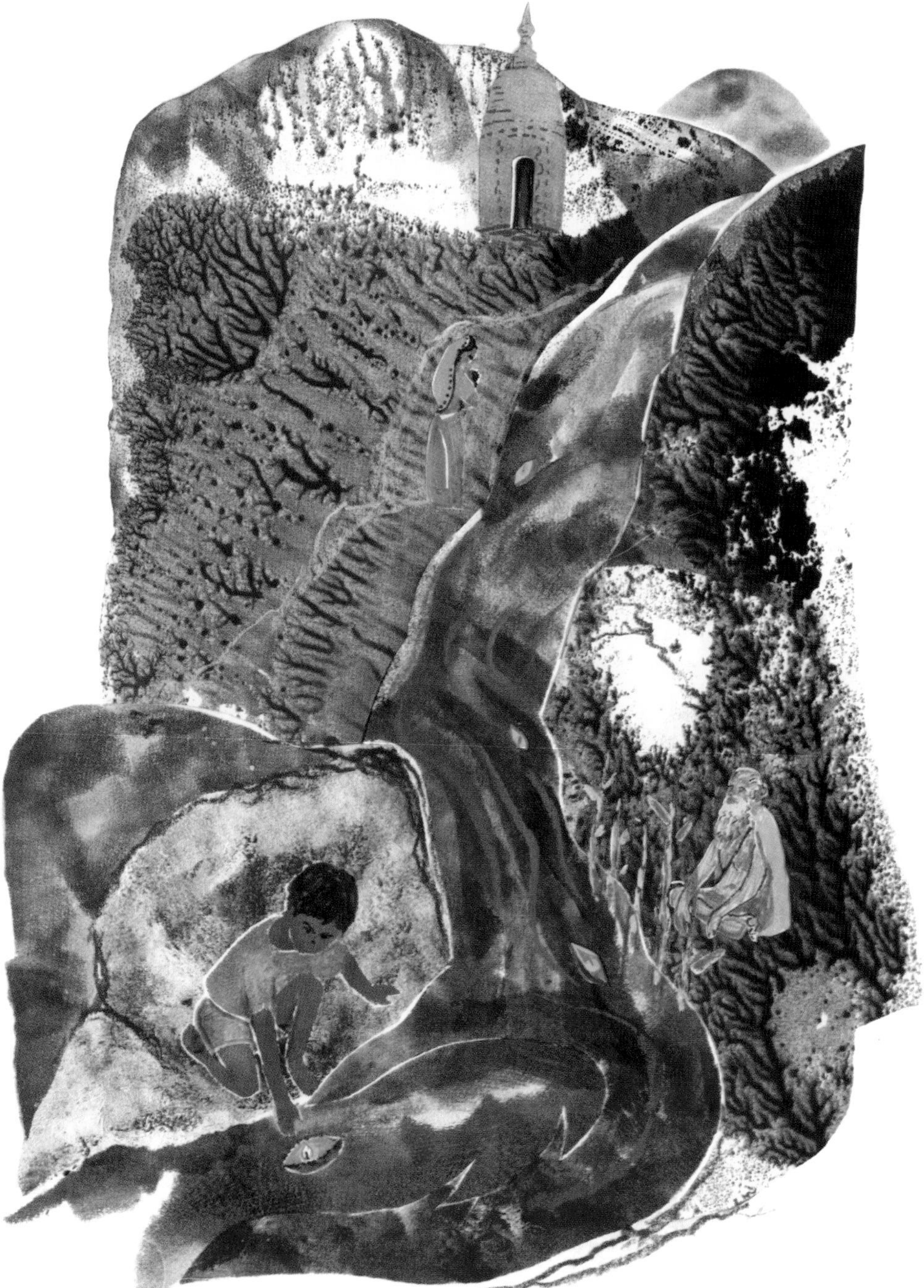

Bhūta Chaturdaśī: Ghost Fourteenth[21]

As the lamps go up
in the gulleys
near Maṇikarṇikā,[22]
you worry about your heartbeat
sudden sneezing, and cold;
you worry about what is hidden
dirt in the corner
dark exerting its will

suddenly lit by the flame
of the swinging light
a dog with one ear runs by
as if there were no death
as if death, like dirt,
were a mother,
helping him paw his way
to the bones

bones are food you say
as the lamps swing
dark licking their flames

you are not food I say
as I pull the shawl tighter
around your collar
and the dog rounds the corner
holding his prize

Śivarātri[23]
(Night of Śiva)

dome
filled with sound
so the sacred tank vibrates
oṃ nama śivāya oṃ namaḥ śivāya
it is not subtle, like slow breath in sleep
its notes are small hands grasping at breasts
sounds push through the dark, demand the flesh of attention

dome
angry with chant
so that sleep collapses
oṃ nama śivāya oṃ namaḥ śivāya
sounds make us rock, and the tanks sway too
we ask the breast of god to hold us like a pillow
curled hands beat out rhythm, and pound for milk and freedom
oṃ namaḥ śivāya oṃ namaḥ śivāya oṃ namaḥ śivāya oṃ namaḥ śivāya oṃ namaḥ

Column of Light,[24] Śivarātri

When the visitors arrived
I ran from the room
where your lights were

the guests sat sumptuous
at a distant table
where fruits, wines soaked them—
and still your candles burned
indifferent to their feeding

meats, breads, piled on the stone
none of them offered to you
as you waited and shone
in the corners behind the wall

I had no time to run back
and smother the flames;
while the guests laughed
I began to think
your fire would destroy
the corners that held you

but when the feeding was done
I went to the room
where your lights stood:
they burned still,
firm and deep pillars,
mocking my doubts

yours pillars of light
do not overwhelm

at the mouths of caverns
and the sheers of cliffs
they just endure
through wanton laughter
and careless feeding—

they just confound
my anxious movements
with stubborn peace

Holi Pūjā

(Festival of bonfires and colored water)[25]

that day
I drove furiously
down Asi road
my ink stained clothes
burned by the wind

with color and speed
you held the world
so my color and speed
were offerings to you

but no-one joined me
no-one noticed
the wheels whirling
my greens, silvers, reds
sailing down the street
I should have known then
when my offering fell
that you usually live
between color and its absence,
between glittering clothes
and the drying burlap
thrown over my wall—

I should have known then
that you are never with qualities
nor are you without them

Kūrma Jayantī, Tortoise Birthday:[26]

On Refusing to be Carried Down the Mountain

(for S.P.)

When I became suddenly tired
and the trees, already ash
looked threateningly white
and the river stones sharpened
in the luscious delirium

you said you would carry me
propped on your back
all the way down the Mandākinī

I refused, held your hand instead
and felt the long fall
into blue and pine
that fainting would bring
as my feet moved forward

you crossed swinging bridges,
touched the bleeding toes
of the grandfather
as he ran to kiss Śiva,
blessed the buses
when they careened around us,
found food in the last ashram
while I, still dignified,
fell asleep on the burlap

but God became a tortoise
because the earth was sinking
he carried it on his back—
a fragile burden
of air and jewels

remembering this,
I still want to say yes
to your asking:
I still want to be
a fragile burden
of air and jewels

Even now I can feel
the rope of your muscle
as your back tightens,
the pines brush my ankles,
and you lift me home.

Buddha Jayantī: Aśoka at Kaliṅga[27]

This weapon
cuts too quickly—
flesh folds and falls
like teak leaves
dropping in monsoon forests
like mangroves
bending to the wind

this weapon
needs an enemy
other than flesh—
other than the chests
of southern princes

perhaps air and breath—
perhaps stone and script—

To swing this weapon
through the air
is to injure myself
in a circle

To swing this weapon
through stone
is to injure myself
in a line

I will breathe differently
bonded to air—
I will write differently
grieving on stone—

then this weapon
will have
better enemies

Part II

Crossings

Fire's Goal

For the Sage Śarabhaṅga[28]

The Rāmāyaṇa reports
your self-combustion
as an act of devotion
since Rāma could not go
to heaven with you
perhaps out of loneliness
you burned yourself
flames came from within
and everyone stared

Eighteenth-century newspapers
told of women who drank
alone in their room
found burned from within
while the furniture
remained untouched
by the flames

longing for god
longing for company
if desire is not met
by substance
it turns back on itself
and the subject burns

breath becomes smoke
flesh becomes flame;
as the body disappears
despair finds relief
in a perfect balance
of its elements

Near-Accident in Front of Viṣṇu's[29] Temple

the wheels caught
in front of the temple
of your many forms

all of you looked on
as the sand careened
toward my face
and the pipes and spokes
lunged forward

unlike you,
i did not have limbs
to catch my balance

as you watched
with white marble eyes
I asked you:
you save the world
in its wheel of pain
what form are you now,
Preserving One,
as you see my flesh
in a storm
of stone and metal?

and then I knew
you took the same form
as the birds
who continue to chirp
after the screeching

has stopped
on the highway

the same form
as the rhododendrons
whose stems push up
ignoring the face
buried beneath them

the same form
that is now cool stone
reminding me
that my intact body
is chance occurrence

the same form
that blesses me
as the wheel rights,
and I move forward
thinking only
of the resolve
of birds and rhododendrons

Camera, Haridwar[30]

Just like the hundreds
of Eskimo words for snow
I remember in tired detail
the stories of the people
who feared a picture
would steal the soul

as you and I exchange malas
and strangers' glances,
you put your feet
into the light water,
god's water, pieces of sky
dished out by the mountain

I raise the lens to focus
and your hand shoots out,
demanding money, laughing

we both know
you will be circulated,
reproduced in basements
and sad lecture halls
where in photo-form
you will no longer demand

your demand
is its own form
of light and intimacy

we both know
once I shoot you
it will not be you
but I, wading after you,
who has lost the soul

Nityaṃ Śeṣa: Viṣṇu's Cobra in the Woods[31]

I want to touch
your scales, your hoods;
I am jealous
of the god
who sleeps on you,
who belches out aeons
like so many yawns
before bed

you approximate infinity—
always in numerals,
and sometimes in feeling

but I also want
to touch those leaves—
the endless traces
of green behind you,
to gather all of them
in small fistfuls
and feel the measure
of my slow feet
padding the dirt
in prayers and circles

these measures
are infinity too,
but they will never
amount to a numeral:

they are instead
the endless counting
of your powers
in sweat and joy

To the king, who remembers Śakuntalā[32]

I envy your ring
found so suddenly
in the belly of a fish:
it is a perfect roundness:
the roundness of memory
seamless passion,
unbroken by journeys
under the waves

there is no fish
to carry this memory
of a lover now gone,
now returned–
the images come
in shards and splinters,
then fragment
into slivers
of light and shade

I envy your ring
as I grasp at them
and they slip
through my fingers
like so many minnows
swimming underfoot

Sūrya Pūjā, Sun Worship

in mid-morning heat
running with dogs
I have left behind
the cool moistness
that separates
the self
from the object
of despair

we are already dry
when the sun shows us
the clean clarity
of attachment:
dogs are the hunt
I am this pain
let them run
let me cry

we are now the day
we no longer hold
the delicate love
of mist and leaf
and darkness

Widow's Bangles on the Gayā River Bed[33]

They glisten by the pyre
as the sun sets
and the smoke rises
a final offering of gray
in the shape of your body

broken in crescents
they shine like doorways
beckoning my grief
to pass through
with the wind
or the last light
in pursuit of your soul.

Hariścandra's Promise to Viśvāmitra[34]

I said to him that I would
and the word held fast
like shining silk
I would I said
because he was burning
and his burning lit me
yes yes yes
my word wound around him
silk woven by a soul
still shaking in its cocoon

now I wash out silks
silks and other cloths
robbed from the dead
because he asked me
because I said yes
I gave him all my light
wife and son paling
in the shine of the beloved word

make the dead clean I say
make this world shine
clean shine clean shine

now flecks of flesh glimmer
as they fall from the cloth
swung against the river rocks
and this soul floats, face down,
in the eddies of silk and water

Sacred Thread,[35] or Spider at Sunrise

ten red petals
and a fly
swing in your web
and you hover
over the expanse
of morning silk
caught between
storage and display

will you eat the petals too,
wrapping the fly
like betel nut?
or will you let them swing
and happily drop
as your web dries?

the soul's work
is to tell the difference
between eating
and contemplation

Śrāddha Offering for a Father[36]

You never liked mangos
they sat on the printed tablecloth
near your elbow
close to your scowl
and the last of the *dahi*

a year after your death
I offer them
with the carnations—
I must honor your aversions
and your silences
and not the shapes
of my own forgetting

mangos hover on the Yamuṇā [37]
as I reassemble your form
in fruits and garlands
and whirls of ashes
congealed in the current

the colors come together
in the backwater;
they form a face,
then disperse,
with no remains
except my longing

this too was the play
of our looks
across the table
when you were alive

On Learning Sacred Language in Childhood

What you remember:
a verb, and how it collided
with a crow,
alighting on the tree
behind your mother's head

a noun, and how it spilled
off the spoon
falling from your brother's mouth

a sentence, and its chill
like the chill of your teacher's hand
on your shoulder

you keep the books
near your body,
they curl and cry
and will not let you
forget their embrace,
their nouns and verbs
break open your silence,
their sentences nag
like children
wanting a drink

you try to quiet them
but they refuse —
the hopes and disturbances
of your wizened sleep

The Guest

"I'll just come in
for a moment,"
she said—
leaving me
no words to reply

but the old etymologist[38]
the rescuer of words
says "a moment"—
the noun *kṣana*—
comes from
the verb "*kṣan*"–
to destroy–

so a "moment"
is a piece of injured time

gashes on the plate
creases in the napkin
stains on the pillow
crumbs near the pipes—
all moments
of injured time

I had no idea
her presence
was a form of infinity

since it was only
tea and raisins
and my reluctant hands

Vinedresser at the Change of Season

in the succulent season
they clung to wood
to my fingers, to each other
any object would do
for green tendrils

now the frost numbs
their grasping
they redden darkly
as they fall
and the wood breathes

in the autumn sun
I cannot tell
if the red
is the color of blood
or of a palm,
slowly opening

Drākṣāmāliko ṛtuparyāye

ṛtau sarase
kāṣṭam vilīyata
aṅgulīr me, anyonyam
kiṃcana dravyaṃ kalpitavyam
haribhyas tantubhyaḥ

himaḥ stabdhīkaroti
teṣāṃ grahaṇam
andhaṃ raktībhavanti
patitvā
kāṣṭaṃ ca śvasiti

na draṣṭuṃ śaknomi
śaradsūrye
yadi raktaṃ
lohitasya varṇaṃ
va hastatalasya
vilambitaṃ vikasato va

For the Red-Throated Sparrow[39]

When the branches rustled,
I was dreaming of Draupadī
singing as she bathed her hair
in Duḥśāsana's blood—
but you wake me with music;
and your red throat reminds me
as Draupadī did
that in some seasons
there is no difference
between beauty and wound.

Raktakaṇthacaṭaka

śākhāsu śakaśakāyantīṣu
svapne draupadīm apaśyaṃ
gayantīṃ snānaṃ kurvatīṃ
śiroruhas tasyā duḥśāsanarakte

gītayā tu māṃ bodhayasi
raktakaṇṭhas te māṃ smārayati
yathā draupadī smārayati
yat keṣucid ṛtuṣu
lāvaṇyena lūnakena
anantaram

Pine Forest

a thin pine shoots up
at the curve in the creek
the light through its needles
sharp as spring
sharp as your question,
Will you wait with me?

Śaralavanam

tanuḥ saraladrumaḥ
udbhinatti
khallakuṭile, sucīṣu ruciḥ
pikānandatīkṣṇaḥ
tīkṣṇas te praśṇa iva—
api pratīkṣase mayā saha
pratīkṣase mayā saheti

Summer Cove in a Time of Loss

the greens here
are too multiple to count;
the tree trunks regulate,
but they are sad afterthoughts
and colors overtake them
lonely brown lines
in a buzz of leaf and water,
their edges, like your silences,
are boundaries drawn too late

Grīṣmakhallaḥ Kṣayakāle

atra palāśāny
atibahudha saṃkhyātum
vṛkṣaskandāḥ kramanti,
viṣaṇṇās tv anubodhāḥ
ragāś ca tāñ jayanty:
asaṅgapiṅgalarekhāḥ
prāntas teṣām, niśabdās ta iva
sīmā likhitā ativilambya

Found Poetry

—for JH

poems found
in the middle of pages
you already knew

khila means:
the holy end
of a sacred text
or the rubble
at the edge of a field

first wisdom:
one's rubbish
is another man's treasure
second wisdom:
it is also one's own

Vittakāvya

kāvyā vittāḥ
madhye patrāṇām
suviditāṇām eva tvayā

khila iti śabdaḥ
pavitrānto vedasya
ucchiṣṭaṃ vā
prānte kṣetrasya
ityarthaḥ

prathamā prajñeti:
puruṣocchiṣṭam
nidhānam antarasyeti
dvitīyā prajñā:
svīyam apīti

Heirloom

my bracelet still hangs
on the bedpost
where you placed it
my earring still dangles
from the sheet
where it fell from your hand

my mother visits
and tells me
I must take better care
of my jewelry

Vaṃśabhojya

Kalayo 'dyāpi me
khatvāstambhe avalambate
yatra tvam eṣam adadhāḥ
karṇiko 'dyāpi me
nicolāl lolati
yatra te hastād agalat

mātābhyāgacchati
māṃ bravīti ca
e manaṃ dhehīti

Notes

Pūrṇimā, Full Moon Sacrifice

Several small sacrifices are performed as auxiliaries to larger Vedic, or early Indian sacrifices. Many of them are still performed today in villages in Andhra Pradesh and traditional Hindu households in Maharashtra. One of the most important of these is the Full Moon sacrifice, which regularly marks the lunar month. The offerings are usually made of rice and milk, cooked and raised up to the moon. These offerings are accompanied by ancient poetic verses called mantras. Much of sacrifice is governed by the idea of linkages, or *bandhu*s, between elements in the universe. In their light-giving qualities and yellowness, there is an essential connection, or *bandhu*, between light, and clarified butter, and fire. So, in offering butter into the fire, one offers what one wants oneself. So, too, in offering the white substances, to the moon, one offers what one longs for in the full moon.

A Full Moon sacrifice in its simple gracefulness reminds one of a moment from *Frannie and Zowie*: that pouring a glass of milk was "God pouring god into god."

Gaṇeśa Bell at Ganeṣotsav

Gaṇeśa is invoked at the beginning of journeys, new ventures, new houses, even new shopping trips. He is a short, fat-bellied figure with an elephanthead, holding a conch-shell in one hand, a revolving disk, a mace, and a waterlily. He is usually found in some niche or other in a temple of Śiva, and at gateways and doorways in homes all over India. His elephant head comes from the fact that his mother, Parvatī, longed for a child, but could not get Śiva, engaged in asceticism, to give her one. She scratched her body before her bath, and from this skin breathed life into this figure. She asked Gaṇeśa a to guard the door of the bathhouse, and when Śiva returned, he did not know his own son, nor did Gaṇeśa know him. A scuffle ensued, and Śiva in his anger lopped off Gaṇeśa's head. Parvatī insisted that her son be restored to life with the first living creature that could be found.

At Gaṇeśa Chaturthi, each town or city is jubilant with processions carrying the image of the god, and every household honors its own image. Gaṇeśa receives a dry pudding of sesame and sugar, and women of the household fast before offering pūjā at moonrise, and tell stories of Gaṇeśa.

At one small corner in Pune, there is a small cafe and a tiny Gane a temple. At that small place a rickshaw driver worships Gaṇeśa everyday. The following is a meditation on what it might be like to integrate the worship of Gaṇeśa into one's daily rickshaw routines of streets and alleys and traffic signals.

Kṛṣṇa Jayantī (Festival of Kṛṣṇa, Cowherd God and Consort of Lovers)

Kṛṣṇa is an avatar of the god Viṣṇu, and is frequently identified with the supreme being himself. His rich mythology spars stories of his birth to Vasudeva and Devakī, his escape from the wicked king Kaṃsa, and his safe childhood raised by the cowherdess Yaśodā and Nanda. Kṛṣṇa is both a hero and a child. His mischievous exploits include stealing butter, vanquishing demoness-nurses, protecting the people of his village Vṛṇdavan against a rainstorm by lifting up a mountain as an umbrella. He also plays and flirts and loves the cowherdesses of Vṛṇdavan, who each feel that they are his chosen one. His love for a cowherdess Rādhā is a model for the relationship between devotee and god. One of the sages Mārkaṇḍeya's visions, as he floats in a cosmic ocean, between the two ages of the world, is of a tiny child, floating on a leaf—that child is Kṛṣṇa. Some seers say that the hero is the fit object of worship for the devotee; some say the child. Kṛṣṇa Jayantī, consists of a fast, often beginning when the moon passes through the asterism of Rohini. The festival ends with the worship of Kṛṣṇa. Some wealthier families worship him as a baby in a swinging cradle, heaped up with garlands of sweet flowers, and surrounded with offerings of milk-products—for which Kṛṣṇa had a particular fondness.

This poem is a meditation on the hero-lover and the child. Just as this combination must be part of the identity of Kṛṣṇa himself, so too it is a part of us as lovers of God and lovers of each other.

Cycle of Hymns to the Goddess

This cycle of hymns to Devī, or the goddess, is a series of poems which describe the multiple ways we might experience a divine mother. Devī has many names in India, and many sides—some inspiring terror and destructive powers, and others inspiring Love, reverence, and comfort. Her various incarnations embody the feminine power of *śaktī*, and her multiplicity attests to the ambiguity and contradictions which *śaktī* entails.

During the festival of Daṣaharā, or "ten day" worship of the goddess, a central image of her is surrounded by lesser deities Sarasvatī, Lakṣmī, and Kartik and Gaṇeśa her sons when she is Parvatī. Every object known to humans is a fit offering; land is offered in a small pot, and the *Devīmahātmya*, the text sacred to the goddess, is recited throughout the nine days and nights. The eighth day is the holiest day, and the goddess' power shines strongest at one particular moment, "as long as a mustard seed can stand on the pointed edge of a cow's horn." Machines, computers, bicycles, automobiles are all festooned with garlands; for they, too have *śaktī*, or female power, which must be honored and preserved. At the end of the festival, in colorful processions, images of the goddess are immersed in bodies of water — tanks, rivers, oceans.

This cycle contemplates the question, "What does multiplicity of Mothers mean?" Mothers are not simply symbols of nurturance, but they are elusive and hard to discern. (Sūrkhaṇḍa Devī) One goddess is associated with the buffalo, and in some places a buffalo is sacrificed to her. In what ways can we learn something about *śaktī* from her association with the heavy low sounds of the buffalo? And what can we learn about her energy when she splits into seven, in her incarnation as the "seven mothers" who help prevent still-birth?

Lakṣmī Pūja (Festival of the Goddess of Wealth)

Lakṣmī, the Goddess of Wealth, is worshiped several different times in the Hindu year. She, like her material counterpart, is part of many families' daily rounds of worship, but her particular festival is after the full moon following Dūrga Pūjā, or Daśaharā. Lakṣmi worship closes a whole fortnight of Devī Pūjā, the worship of the Goddess.

Lakṣmī makes her circuit around the entire globe during the night of her worship, and gives wealth to anyone who is awake. One drinks coconut juice and keeps awake during this night. Before the vigil, a leafy canopy is built over a figure of the goddess, and a small copper jug is placed to her side, and she is painted with red ochre or sandal paste. The oldest married woman of the house keeps a fast on this day on behalf of the whole household, and then makes offerings of flowers, fruits and sweets to the goddess. Coconut and flattened rice are among her favorite offerings, and she rides on an owl. Cowry shells, perhaps an early form of currency, are also a favorite of Lakṣmi's. Household ceremonies of Lakṣmī pūjā, with all of their efflorescence, make one wonder about the ways in which wealth makes circuits around the globe.

Dīwālī at Gangotri

Dīwālī's origins are numerous. It is now called the Hindu new year, and is marked by many days of gift-giving, presentation of saris, the honoring of brothers and sisters, and feasting. One story tells the victory of Viṣṇu over the demon Bali who was terrifying the world with his ascetic powers. Taking the form of a dwarf Vāmana, Viṣṇu begged the demon Bali to allow him a small plot of land: whatever he could cover in three steps. Bali, being merciful, allowed this, at which point, Viṣṇu transformed himself into a giant. In the first step, he covered the earth, in the second the atmosphere, and in the third, for lack of anywhere to step, Viṣṇu stepped on Bali's head, thus returning Bali to the underworld.

Another basis for Dīwālī comes from the Hindu epic, the Rāmāyaṇa. In that epic, the demon Rāvaṇa captures Rāma's wife Sītā. Rāma is a human avatar of Viṣṇu, especially created to rid the world of Rāvaṇa who, like Bali, has a greedy energy that puts him in fierce competition with the gods. Rāma travels to Laṅka, Rāvaṇa's abode, and in the ensuing battle kills the demon and frees Sītā. Dīwālī celebrates this freedom and the crowning of Rāma upon his return to his city of Ayodhya.

Dīwālī's connections with light are numerous and delightful. Some light lamps in order to avoid falling again under the demon Bali's power. Others light them in order to show thier deceased ancestors the way to heaven, still others to avoid a violent death. Some simply wave lighted lamps in order to honor the natural beauty of water.

Śivarātri

While this is a special night, the worship of Śiva is a simple and everyday act in almost all parts of India; it involves pouring water on a liṅgam—the representation of Śiva in a raised stone, symbolic of fertility, male virility, and creative power itself. Śiva is a complex being with both creative and destructive powers; he is a householder with a beautiful wife Parvatī and two children, as well as an ascetic who meditates for ages on end, wandering amongst the cremation grounds and the wilderness. Śiva's energy might best be described as the process of transformation itself involving both destruction and creation.

On Śivarātri, one fasts for a day abstaining from both food and drink, and at night worship the god Śiva, either in their own house or a nearby Śiva temple. The temple priest makes offerings and chants on behalf of family and one's own needs. Śivarātris are often sleepless due to the chanting from nearby temples. In such states of insomnia one begins to think about the ways in which Śiva's powers of creation and destruction are contained in the very sounds of his chants.

Holi Pūjā (Festival of Bonfires and Colored Water)

The beginnings of the Holi festival are numerous as the ways it is celebrated. It occurs at the end of the month of Phalgun, on the full moon, which coincides roughly with March. In the early morning, bonfires are lit all over villages in India, symbolizing the victorious destruction of a flesh-eating demoness named Holikā—hence the name Holi for the holiday. Holikā could also have been the wicked aunt of a famous devotee Kṛṣṇa, who tried to kill him but was only burned herself in the flames. When the bonfire is built all the villagers contribute something to it—wood, cowdung cakes, broken pieces of furniture for fuel.

Holi has been embraced by villagers and anthropologists alike as the rituals of inversion, and merry chaos, where children play tricks on their elders, employees on bosses, the less powerful on the rulers of the village. *Rang khelna*, or playing with colors, is a crucial part of this chaos. People run from house to house, squirting and splashing each other with colored water and powder.

When celebrating Holi, covered with ink, one wonders whether in god's eyes the colors served to disguise or reveal.

Fire's Goal

According to the Rāmāyaṇa epic (Āraṇyakandha 4.18-36), the sage Śarabhaṅga has won the world of Brahmā by his fierce austerities. But the sage had delayed leaving the earth for the realm of Brahmā until he had laid eyes on Rāma. Soon Rāma and Sītā visit him as he is performing a fire sacrifice, and he entertains them as honored guests. The sage Śarabhaṅga asks him to accept all the worlds he has won, and Rāma replies that he hopes to win these worlds for himself. Rāma then asks the sage to show them a place to dwell in the forest. Śarabhaṅga gives then directions, and then asks R ma to stay for a while and watch as he abandons his body, like a snake abandons its worn out skin. Śarabhaṅga enters the fire, is burned, and takes on the form of radiant youth. He then ascends to the world of Brahmā, who welcomes him heartily.

To the King, Who Remembers Śakuntalā

A descendant of the great lunar sages, King Duṣyanta dwelled in Hastinapura as his capital. He was a companion of Indra in many battles against the demons. akuntal was the daughter of Viśvāmitra and the celestial woman Menakā. Menakā was sent by Indra to tempt Viśvāmitra away from his spiritual austerities, which were threatening to make the Viśvāmitra more powerful than Indra himself. Viśvāmitra succumbed to the temptation and Śakuntalā was born from their union. Raised in the forest by the sage Kaṇva as her foster father, Śakuntalā saw the king Duṣyanta on a hunting expedition, and both fell in love. The two performed a self-marriage, lived together and produced a child. When Duṣyanta left for Hastinapura he promised to return for her and gave her a ring of remembrance. All alone in the forest, Śakuntalā began to pine for King Duṣyanta. When great sage Durvāsa came to pay a visit at her door, she was unaware of his presence and did not attend to him. The sage was angry at her inattention and cursed her to be forgotten by the one she thought of most — i.e. Duṣyanta. The curse would be broken only by a token of recognition.

When Śakuntalā's foster-father Kaṇva returned, he was pleased to hear of her marriage to Duṣyanta and sent her to Hastinapura. King Duṣyanta, under the spell of forgetfulness, did not recognize Śakuntalā when she arrived. Her ring, the token that would break the spell, had gone missing, and Śakuntalā went away in defeat. A few days later, a fisherman then came to King Duṣyanta, accused of having tried to sell a ring that he had found in the belly of a fish. It was Śakuntalā's ring, and upon seeing it, King Duṣyanta remembered Śakuntalā. He became deeply ashamed that he had shunned his wife. Eventually the king returned to the hermitage where akuntal lived with her foster-father Kaṇva and her child by King Duṣyanta. Duṣyanta recognized the child, and Śakuntalā saw the ring—her ring—on King Duṣyanta's hand. The two were happily reunited and returned to Hastinapura. The foster-father sage Kaṇva predicted that their son would grow up to be an all powerful king—king Bharata—and rule over all of India.

Sacred Thread at Sunrise

All who study the sacred texts of the Vedas undergo the *upanayana* ritual, or donning of the sacred thread. It symbolizes a commitment to cleanliness and purity anad spiritual discipline. The sacred thread is as natural to a twice-born, or initiated person, as his body. Since it is both a symbol of a ritually created person and a natural state, it is intriguing to think of forms of sacred threads within nature as well as within ritual. The holiday of Śravaṇi Pūrṇimā, brahmins and others renew the sacred thread. They rise at dawn, bathe and put on white garments. They perform a fire sacrifice, offering rice balls and casting their old threads into the fire. Eight rows of *darbha* grass represent the original seven sages and Arundhatī, at the creation of the world. They reconsecrate their new threads with recitation of the Gāyatrī mantra, one of the most auspicious Vedic verses.

Footnotes

[1] Pūrṇimā is a ritual of offerings to the moon at the start of the lunar month, usually made of rice and milk.

[2] At this festival, in late monsoon August, snakes are honored with offerings; neighbors find local ponds and wells to bathe in, and make drawings on doorposts and thresholds. One legend has it that the famous grammarian Patañjali, is descended from a family of *nāgas*, or snakes.

[3] Gaṇeśa, the son of Śiva and Parvatī, is celebrated on the Fourth Day of the Waning Moon of Magh—usually in September. He has a rotund body with an elephant's head, and is known as the Remover of Obstacles, or more positively, the Giver of Success.

[4] Kṛṣṇa is one of the most pan-Indian of gods, and is a child prankster, a coherd hero, and a lover. His festival occurs on the waning fortnight of Bhadra (around August). During the time between the great cycles of ages, Kṛṣṇa floats in the cosmic ocean as a mounainous body of a child floating on a leaf.

[5] Dūrga Pūjā, the worship of the goddess, lasts for nine days and nine nights; thus it is called Navarātri and occurs in the moonlit half of the months of Aśvin (September-October). She is worshipped in all her manifestations during Navarātri. during the year the Divine Mother is celebrated in both presence and absence, as suggested by these poems.

[6] Vedic hymns, composed around 1500 BCE. The goddess is said to predate the composition of these traditional Sanskrit verses.

[7] The buffalo is associated with the goddess in many myths, and some rituals in parts of southern India.

[8] A minor pilgrimage site devoted to the goddess Sūr Khaṇḍa Devī, located near the Himalayan town of Dhanolti.

[9] Videhā, after having given birth to eight children who died, took shelter in the shrine of a goddess, and was granted her wish to give birth to living children. The woman who keeps this festival must make eight water pots,

and place on top of them the flour images of the seven *mātṛis*, or mothers, and worship them by name.

[10] Goddess of eloquence.

[11] Goddess of music, especially cymbals.

[12] Goddess of warfare.

[13] Goddess of spells and magic.

[14] Goddess wife of Vārāha, the boar *avatāra* of Viṣṇu who held up the earth.

[15] Goddess wife of Indra, a trickstress.

[16] Goddess of leatherworkers and other menial labors.

[17] Dīwālī, usually October/November, is the festival of triumph of light over darkness. At twilight in Dīwālī, small leaves containing lamps are floated down the river. If it floats safely downstream, the year will be happy. Gangotri is the town nearest the source of the Ganges River in the Himalayas.

[18] Dīwālī celebrates Viṣṇu, in the form of a dwarf, defeats the demon Bali.

[19] Dīwālī marks Rāma rescuing his wife Sītā and defeating the demon Rāvaṇa.

[20] A traditional Hindu renunciant and forest-dweller who practices meditation.

[21] Yama the king of the Dead told the citizens of Varanasi that the lighting of lamps every evening, from Aśvina kṛṣṇa 13th to Kārttika śukla 2nd, would avert a sudden and violent death.

[22] In Varanasi, Maṇikarṇikā is the main *ghat*, or riverside sacred place, where bodies are cremated. This place is considered to be both highly auspicious and highly polluted.

[23] Śivarātri is a religious fast, and the name of the holiday means "the night consecrated to iva." It occurs on the Fourteenth day of the dark half of Phalgun, coinciding with February/March. Śiva is a complex god withboth creative and destructive powers, a householder and an ascetic at the same time.

[24] Śiva frequently appears in a column of light, called a *jyotirliṅgam*, or *liṅgam* of light. These appearances are usually in dramatic natural places, such as a waterfall, a cave, or a mountain forest. Yet Śiva's nature is such that they might also appear in more domestic spaces, such as a dinner party.

[25] Holi occurs on the full moon of Phalgun, roughly in March. Celebrations involve the lighting of bonfires to celebrate the victory over the demoness Holika. Neighbors, friends, and family squirt colored water on each other during the holiday, a time of social inversions and chaos.

[26] Kūrma Jayantī occurs in the month of Vaiśākha, April/May. Viṣṇu became a tortoise to hold up the mountain Mandara during the demons' and gods' churning of the ocean. Thanks to the tortoise, Mount Mandara could act as a kind of churn dasher for the sacred act of churning.

[27] King Aśoka converted to Buddhism in the 3rd century BCE, after a particularly bloody battle at Kalinga, in the forested and coastal state of Orissa in eastern India. His stone pillar edicts, outlining Buddhist practice and ethics, are found all over India.

[28] According to the Hindu epic the Rāmāyaṇa, the sage Śarabhaṅga waited to see Rāma, an incarnation of the god Viṣṇu, before immolating himself in a fire and ascending to heaven.

[29] Viṣṇu's way of being is to preserve the world and protect it from disaster. He takes many forms, called *avatarā*s, in order to accomplish these feats.

[30] Haridwar is the place where the River Ganges hits the plains from the mountains. As in many Hindu holy places, it is populated by riverside merchants selling supplies for worship, such as flowers, coconuts, and incense.

[31] Viṣṇu is said to recline on an ocean between the ages, protected by a snake whose spread hood hovers over his head. This snake, or *śeṣa,* is a symbol of infinity and endless power that the god possesses.

[32] Śakuntalā is a maiden born of celestial beings who is cursed by a sage. Her doom is to be forgotten by the one who loves her–King Duṣyanta. King Duṣyanta's memory of his great love Śakuntalā suddenly comes back through a fisherman, who is brought before the king for stealing a ring he accidentally finds in a fish. That ring is Śakuntalā's.

[33] It is customary for some Hindu widows to break their bangles by the side of their husbands' funeral pyres, as a sign of the dissolution of earthly bonds.

[34] Hariścandra the king was bound to fulfill a vow to the sage Viśvāmitra. In order to meet the sage's increasing demands, the king gave his kingdom, wife, and son. The king himself took work as washerman at the cremation ground by the river, stealing clothes from bodies and reselling them clean.

[35] A brahmin will usually wear a sacred thread over his right shoulder as a sign of being "twice-born"–initiated into the world of Vedic learning. Ideally, the sacred thread commits him to spiritual discipline and moderation.

[36] *Śraddha* is the offering for an ancestor, the previous generations to whom one owes one's life. From ancient India onwards, a *śraddha* has consisted of balls of rice and water. They can also consist of fruit and incense. One can also make an offering on the anniversary of a recent death in the family.

[37] The Yamuṇā is one of the three most sacred rivers in North India, along with the Gaṅgā (Ganges), and the Sarasvatī, a river which has gone underground.

[38] Yāska authored the *Nirukta*, a Sanskrit etymological dictionary from the 5th century BCE. Even then, few people knew the meanings of words which were daily used in ritual, and he attempted to find origins for words based on similarity of sound.

[39] In the Hindu epic the *Mahābhārata*, the heroine Draupadī is wife of the five Paṇḍava brothers. She suffers public humiliation at the hands of Duḥśāsana, one of the Kaurava brothers who are the Paṇḍava's enemies. She swears that she will wash her hair in his blood out of revenge for the abasement she has suffered. [25] Holi occurs on the full moon of Phalgun, roughly in March. Celebrations involve the lighting of bonfires to celebrate the victory over the demoness Holikā. Neighbors, friends, and family squirt colored water on each other during the holiday, a time of social inversions and chaos.

Laurie L. Patton

Laurie L. Patton earner her BA from Harvard University and her PhD from the University of Chicago. Since 1984 she has made her Indian homes in Varanasi and Pune. She has published *Authority, Anxiety, and Canon: Essays in Vedic Interpretation* (1994); *Myth as Argument: The Bṛhaddevatā as Canonical Commentary* (1996); *Myth and Method* (1996); and *Jewels of Authority: Women and Textual Tradition in Hindu India* (2002). She is currently completing a book on the use of poetry in Vedic ritual, *Bringing the Gods to Mind*, and her translation of the *Bhagavad Gita* is forthcoming from Penguin Press. She is Chair of the Department of Religion, Emory University. Her poems have appeared in local literary journals in Chicago, Atlanta, Pune, and Jerusalem; she was also awarded the University of Chicago Prize for Best Poetry in 1987.

Lika Tov

Lika Tov was born in Amsterdam, the Netherlands, where she studied graphic art at the Rietveld Academy. After immigrating to Israel she specialized in printmaking and developed new techniques (collagraphs, monoprints, etc.). The illustrations in this book are a combination of collages of textured papers, prepared as part of an experiment with paints and printing ink, stencil printing (oil paint), and lines drawn with color pencils and pens. Her other illustrations include *The Arabian Nights* (in Hebrew; Jerusalem; Kiryat Sefer, 1980); *A Story About Elephants* (in Hebrew and Arabic; 1980); *Op Weg [On the Way]—Stories from the Bible for Children* (Dutch; Meinema, 1993).

Narendra Panjwani

Narendra Panjwani is a cultural critic, journalist, and scholar of film currently residing in Bombay. He is Head of the Film Archive, at Osian's Art Company, Bombay. In the fall of 1999 he was a visiting professor at the University of California, Berkeley, and in 1998, a resident scholar at the National Center for the Humanities, North Carolina. He received his Ph.D. in urban sociology from Bombay University in 1984, and was a featured columnist at *The Times of India* for the next ten years, writing on the literatures, cultures, and religions of India. He has also made 22 short films for children on mathematics, history, and geography. His book, *Indian Teenagers and the Hindi Movie Experience*, is in press.